Ramble Young Girl Ramble

A Collection
of
Poetry & Anecdotes

Monique Lorden
1985Poet

Ramble Young Girl Ramble copyright © 2019 amended in 2021 by Monique Lorden. All rights reserved. No part of this book may be used or reproduced in any manner whatsoever without written permission from the author with the exception of quotations in the context of articles, reviews, or other approved publishing.

www.1985poet.com
1985poet@gmail.com
Publisher: 1985POET LLC
ISBN: 978-0-578-67988-4
Library of Congress Control Number: 2020907171
Illustrated by: Diana Ejaita & Monique Lorden
Special Thanks to Mirza Gohar Nayab
INSTAGRAM: @1985POET | TWITTER: @1985POET

Words from a woman who thought she had no business writing.
A woman who will always dance in grace and fight to be heard.

For my daughter and son who listened to me ramble on with questionable interest and unwavering support. For my mother and father who watched me cry tears of pain and joy and consoled me with their love. For all those who know and few who may not know these words are because of our experience.

To the soul reading this,
My heart and Black skin have some things to tell you. Placing emotions between browns and midnight blues between incorrect grammar and bold thoughts I want you to know wrongs will be right. It will be ok. We do not bloom from poplar trees. We are strength. We are resilience. We are hope. The rebellion inside of us birthed the revolution that is us many moons ago.

Love,
Monique Lorden

RAMBLE YOUNG GIRL RAMBLE

"*Ramble Young Girl Ramble* is a literary exhibition of Monique Lorden's calling as a poet and interdisciplinary artist. She gives us depth and color through words and bold illustrations while leaving room to breathe. This collection is her canvas. Her use of poetry with illustrations tell stories while holding their own independently. You will feel the intention. *Ramble Young Girl Ramble* is catered to every experience while highlighting forgiveness, healing, and Black exceptionalism. It is truly powerful."

— *Community Arts Collective*

"'*If not cared for properly, that mystery turns into uncertainty and, naturally, uncertainty translates to insecurity*', the internal rhyming that's infused in your honesty is breath taking. - Yet, it's real and straight forward. Very Nikki Giovanni-esque. Once I read, '*this is my self-love journey*' I knew that I was going to fall in love with your book! It is so imperative to not only practice self-love, but to also read about it! We need to see how others do it for inspiration an insight. With self-love comes accountability and self-awareness. Glad to see it in your collection."

"I'm gonna write like her when I grow up."

— *Jasmine Harrell,*
author of Long Live Phoenixes and Release

"*Ramble Young Girl Ramble* is a masterpiece to mastering peace. It is a cultural necessity and experience of heartbreak, healing, and love. Monique Lorden is an author of wordplay. I took this journey of *Love Lost* and *Love After Love*... and found myself inspired to use everyday words in the most creative ways. Genius! Poetry is and it isn't. Poetry clarifies and *RYGR* does just that. It stands strong in print and as spoken word. This is a paragon of poetry and Lorden is not on her way, she is here. Bend your pages. Bookmark them. Spend time with them. Find yourself in them. Dig your way out of them."

— *Southern Poets*
A collection of authors and works

RAMBLE ON

BY MONIQUE LORDEN

A Wish for Freedom - Poetry Journal
I Wish for Freedom - Children's Picture Book
Ramble Young Girl Ramble - Poetry and Prose

RAMBLE YOUNG GIRL RAMBLE

EStd 1985

This is dedicated to the woman I used to be.
May I never forget you.
May I always bring you flowers.

Unrooted from soil my ancestors called home.
Roots becoming a trace of lineage.
From glorious triumph and open hearts.
Shifting hardened dirt and lovely bones.
Deliberate proof that growth is my birthright.
Reminding me to bloom in every way.
Evidence that it was tireless palms
and residual psalms
that require me to water me
to be the tree and the seed,
to be the flower and the foliage.

RAMBLE YOUNG GIRL RAMBLE

RYGR

WOMEN KNOW SACRIFICE,
FOR WE ARE MADE IN GOD'S IMAGE.
OUR BODIES HOLY TO BRING LIFE.
OUR HEARTS PURE TO BRING LOVE.
THERE IS NO DISTINCTION BETWEEN THE TWO.
YOU ARE A WOMAN RAISED BY A WOMAN RAISING A WOMAN.
THE CHALLENGE TO REVOLUTIONIZE THE WORLD WITH LOVE
WAS ACCEPTED ON YOUR BEHALF MANY MOONS AGO
BY WOMEN WHO SAW GIANTS TREMBLE AT YOUR WHISPER
AND GENTLE WINDS BOW TO YOUR ROAR.
KEEP RAMBLING YOUNG GIRL.
KEEP DREAMING YOUNG GIRL.
FOR NOT MANY THINGS CAN COMPETE WITH DREAMS OTHER
THAN WISHES AND WORDS.
THEY ALL HAVE THE POWER TO PUT YOU IN PLACES YOU COULD
ONLY IMAGINE.
YOU WILL BIRTH NATIONS.
YOU WILL FREE HEARTS.

I am mostly alone and have always been, even in the company of another. Although predictable, my life is surrounded by mystery. If not cared for properly, that mystery turns into uncertainty and, naturally, uncertainty translates to insecurity. My insecurities are always internal. The world watches, but never sees. Velious eyes and a jealous heart. I've mastered emancipation from mental servitude, yet I still fight for liberation. I could write a book on it. ***A Wish For Freedom,*** that's what I'll call it. I am a creative introvert and socially awkward, yet somehow touch souls with my words. They call it poetry. Through art: I am fearless. I could leap mountains with the stroke of my paint brush. I dream in water colors, yet am only skilled with acrylics. I love flowers, but never had the courage to plant them. I am learning to love the in-between.

> I have books inside of me that will birth nations, we all do.
> This is my self-love journey.

PROTECT YOUR PEACE

In the last of years, God made way for a reawakening of sorts. There are days when my mind wanders and I dream of the day I would be in my current state of bloom, thanking God that along the way, He protected my peace and guarded my heart.

Stay soft

Beautiful girl you were made soft to handle all the hard things.
Oh, the irony

To the lover I lost along the way

You claimed territory to my body.
Taught me love.
Taught me lies.
Your filthy mouth spoke honeyed words
boy, were they the sweetest sounds.
I didn't see my father in you
and you were fatherless.
No example of a man-
no desire to be one.
That didn't slow me down-
I was 18.

I was 18 when I promised you my body.
Too young to understand that promises are meant to be
kept
and promises are hard to keep.
You laid with me.
You lied with me.
You were inside of me.
Inside of my body sooner than my heart.
I liked it.
I didn't understand it but I liked it.
Words I couldn't define,
so I called it,
Love

                                      We called it 13 years and 2 children.
                                           Sorry for the pain I caused
                                 by defining words I did not understand.

2 Understandings
Love Lost
Love After Love After Love

2 Understandings
Love Lost
Love After Love After Love
2 Understandings

Understanding 1
Love Lost

back back gimme 6 feet

Bury me in silk,
bury me in satin,
in gold.
Bury me in free land.
Bury me in a love that never was,
like open casket goodbyes,
you held my heart one last time.
6 feet underwhelmed by your last reprise.
I was dead to you
While you live on as a love that never was.

He never gave me flowers.
I never asked for them.
It wasn't until I realized
I didn't need his flowers,
that I began to bloom.

Each petal plucked a lesson.
He loves me,
he loves me knot.

He never showed me so.

Lost in creation

I am the colors on the brush he couldn't ignore.
Trouble is, I used my canvas to paint his story
leaving no room for me.
Creating color on the edge of sanity,
outside of the lines of integrity.
Giving my soul to the soul-less,
four walls made a home
and I was homeless.
With nowhere to go,
no courage to say:
I remember who I was before I met you.
So, I live in the remembrance of yesterday,
when my canvas was fact
to where I've been
and where I'm goin'

Deadlines and dead lines

A writer blocked causes writer's block.
Deadlines causing dead lines,
unrequited love being the only thing she could pen.

Dissolution may not be the solution
and divorce ain't easy,
but a girl's got to choose.
Choice ain't never been my thing.
Shuddering from my lips
I whisper

I

CHOOSE

ME

I CHOOSE ME

JUJU MAN

Beautiful clemency
dripping like honey from her lips.
Forgiveness was but a sweet surprise.
She forgives me,
She forgives me knot.
I was tied to her
like vows of forever.
Pendants on our fingers,
kisses with aftertaste
memories still linger.
I was tied to her.
I loved her
and I lied to her.
Took parts of her.
Discarded her.
Took parts of her
like hearts and nerves
and things that made her feel
she had a soul.
I took that too.
A beautiful soul.
A soul that made her glow and fold
to the inadequacies of me.
How selfish.
Leaving her bare and barren
to a life supposed.
She still found room to grow and hold
a place in her heart to forgive.
She forgives.
She forgives me.
She forgives me not.

$12 \div 4 =$ *me, myself, and I*

Sometimes you will leave
and other times,
it will be them.
Never retrace steps
to a path
not worth journeying again.
Revolving doors
and open hearts
are two in the same.
Be ready for what
you may let back in
again and
again and
again.

        They say 4 is a lucky number
        and 3 preludes completion
        and 12...
        Well that number
        is just the dividend
        and this...
        maybe this is just a mathematical distraction,
        to subtract your mind off of him,

or her
or them.
It's easier that way.
It allows the healing to begin
and forgiveness to take course.
For grievance and remorse to ensue.
For your path to become clear.
For inner work that's overdue.
So, when you leave
or when its them,
never retrace steps
to a path
not worth journeying again.
Instead, count your blessings
in the lessons,
because the distance you traveled
is far from the affliction
of where you've been.

Pawning unsanctified gold and stones
enough to pay rent.
Perhaps, it's what I owe
for keeping the wolf from the door.
For existing here
in a space I don't belong.
Don't be long.
Don't be long.
These heels is howling.
The dust has settled.
My skin is quiet.
The truth is loud.
My pride is gone.
I tell myself as I spin the turnstile
wedding rings ain't worth much no more.
Gold turns green with time.

Definition of *keep the wolf from the door*
Informal | Sho' feels formal when you don't have

: to have or earn just enough money to afford things
that are needed to survive, like food and clothing.
They make just enough to *keep the wolf from the door.*

Why are we taught to unlove
when love doesn't last?
We unlove the one we once adored,
we unlove ourselves.

BREATHE.

Continue to love in the presence of loss,
especially when you may not understand
which love you are unloving.

Loss ain't always a loss
consider it a gain
when the lesson is a blessing
and life goes on
because life will always go on.
The pains will wane,
the tears that once stained
the cheeks of a foreign smile,
will wade away too.

Buried in waters of renewal and hope,
you will be reborn.
Baptized to a life of purpose and prose,
a sacrament of sacrifice,
you will be reminded of who you are.
Rendering stories of what was and what will be.
Allow the water to cultivate what they thought they buried
and bloom every part of your being.
Glory in the garden that God is creating.
Find peace in the petals plucked
and hope in your roots that run deep.
Know who you are.
Who you are destined to be.
Never forgetting
never mistaking
that you are worth anything
less than-

free.

My dear soul:
Remember,
when the lesson is a blessing
and life goes on,
your pain was your path to renewal
and the lesson is a part of your song.
Wade in your troubled waters
as you travel and journey along
to a place of peace and purpose-
one you will deservingly

call home.

I wonder if heaven got a ghetto.
If come as you are welcomes me as I am.
If it's free before 10
and my Papa is there.

My grandma told your grandma
never dim your light or your fire.
My grandma told your grandma
never lose hope or desire.
My grandma told your grandma
when it rains it always showers.
My grandma told your grandma
the rain will bloom your flowers.
Humming hymns under angels' breath
house slippers tapping cracked vinyl
sweeter than any record I ever heard.
My grandmothers could deliver a word.
A sermom.
A prayer.
A testimony of truth.
I knew them before any scripture.
Two creams and coffee as Black as them
with strength to carry generations.
I can hear them say, Hey Suga whatcha need?
So, allow me to let this poem breathe.
Inhale and exhale the what-ifs.
Allow me to let this poem seed.
I never knew my grandmothers.
Both departed before I truly arrived.
I dream of their cadence
and wonder if they were poets.
If their words spoke me into existence.
If their arms lift me in continuance.
If I am because of them.
I am because of them.
This is for them.

Time lives on my face.
I enjoy aging.
It means I am living.
I enjoy seeing my friends start
families and live their purpose.
It means they are leaving legacy.
I enjoy seeing our new grey hairs
and bodies needing rest.
It means we are alive.

Home is where the ××art is

Home ain't in the four walls that cover you.
Freedom ain't in the absence of institutions
that smother you.
Find both in communities that look like you
and love on you
and people who shine wisdom like the sun
on you.

Shine on em'

Home is in the hearts of the free.

Free

And freedom is home to you and you and
you.
Remember, you are greater than the
mistakes of your past memories,
those choices don't stop you from being
free.
Your story ain't over.
You are writing it as we speak.
Second chances are earned
and this dirt road ain't meant for the weak,
but for those who are purposed,
for those who are the seed.

I keep my poetry close to my heart. Inches from life and less than. Close enough that blurred lines and heart strings are one and the same. In a place where rejection found space to exist. Fortunately, the heart is one of the strongest muscles in the body. Resilient. Able to handle love, heartache, and rejection. Able to know that when the beat fades and love becomes an afterthought, the mind tells the body it's time to keep fighting and the beat lives on.

Bones don't hold me together.
I've been broken too many times,
pieced back together by love and
God's embrace.
A poet's frame nonetheless.
Body held by words
bound by mind and emotion,
pressed together like the pages of a book.
Closed to the world.
Open to imagination.
Slave to the pen.
Free to the ink.
Working for no man.
Finding what was lost,
losing what they seek.
Liberated to peace,
enclosed by ideas.
Frank to the oceans,
deity to the seas.
Writing for our future,
speaking for harmony
and unity
and unity
and unity.
Bones don't hold me together
I am not this body.
I am a soul
that lives on
in the words
and grows eternal
in the pages
of my poetry.

He never gave me flowers.
Instead, I collected my own.
I bloomed an awful garden
filled with forget-me-knots
pruned by unkempt hands
and an unkept heart.

FREE

Father forgive us
for the sins we hold gently in the palms of our hands.
Clutching them safe from your redemption.
Mend us and make us whole.
Allow us to remember
to honor the fragments,
for our light still shines through the cracks of what is
and our light still gleams through the seams of what was.
Free our hands.
Never let go.
We need to believe in freedom.
We need to believe in freedom.

LIBRA'S INDECISION

Freedom's rent is due
and she's got none.
Displacing emotions,
retracing emotions,
staying away from the pain of unendurable places.
Sharing shelter with misery and hope.
She prayed for a better today
because she does not believe in tomorrow.

Declined

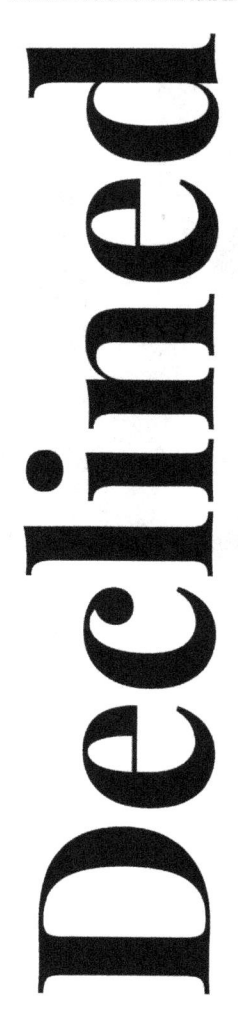

I paid you on time.
Sealed my soul in an envelope
to the only address I knew:

Home.
Penned you a letter
to take the pain away
from an ache overdue.
I gave you all of me
and parts of me
wholeheartedly.

Hope.
I gave you that too
and yet you asked for more.
A currency I didn't have to give
a word I could no longer define.
I was broke
and broken
and over being over it.
Yet, you wanted more of me.
So, instinctively
I wrote one letter more
in scarlet letters and blues.
Emotions inked on scattered sheets
spelling
pain in full refused.

Saṃsāra

When I was a child, my mother told me I was an artist. She saw a creative light inside me, a light she knew would bring others hope as it brought her. She bought my first easel, put me in lessons, and encouraged me to write. Years later, my mother saw that light go out. I stopped creating. I lost faith. I lost hope. I stopped loving myself; and without love there was no desire to live. Theoretically, I died a few times; and even in death I chose life. I chose life, and in choosing life I chose love. Baptized by the grace of the Most High, I understood the relevance of death and that temporary is as beautiful as permanence. I live to allow parts of me to die for rebirth to begin. My father told me I was a revolutionary, that I would change the world with love. Theoretically, I had to die a few times. I had to bury pieces of me to understand that. To welcome it. To love myself the way God intended. To see that by changing me, I've already revolutionized the world.

It takes a divine element of strength
to admit you considered suicide
and no longer reside in the place
that made you dance with danger.
Mama, I'm sorry you find out this way.
Find out that I did not love myself the way you hoped.

Game Over

You broke my heart into pieces
in the most puzzling of ways
and still I hoped you'd peace me together.
My god couldn't mend what shattered.
I cried for you.
I cried for my life.
Told you my darkest secret.
The piece of the puzzle that never fit.
Told you I wish I didn't exist.
You didn't listen.
Your silence said,
try it, you'll never be enough.
It was a brief escape from those moments
where I'm glad
I never called your bluff.

WAR+LOVE
WAR−
WAR+LOVE

This is not poetry. These are not just words. This is me telling you that I am who I am because of hurt and pain. If you listen close enough, you'll hear truth between rhythmic breaks and rhythmic breakdowns. You'll hear me tell you that love ain't easy; love after love exists; and even in knowing that my love ain't perfect, my heart is all in.

I never understood why I fought for a love
that never fought for me.
Then I remembered
there is no room for love in war.

WAR+LOVE

Beautiful girl,

you were made soft to handle all the hard things. Dear Lord, the irony. I would keep a count of the times I cried until I lost count. Tears watered the hard exterior that I became. I remember crying when my brother joined the military. As if his decision to fight for a country that never fought for him was an escape from Black men fighting on familiar soil. I cried again when I dropped out of law school. I cried when I lost my grandfather, the eldest thread that held us all together. I cried when I gained a child. And, each time he called me out of my name, I cried before, after, and in between and no one knew these things. Oh, how I am soft. My body is soft. My thighs are soft. My breasts are soft. My voice is soft. I am sensitive to both the touch and tongue. I pray that those around me catch on to this, but treat me no different. Because unlike most, I was made soft to handle all the hard things.

I end up wiping rivers like I left the water runnin'. Ain't no lovin' here. Ain't no lovin' here.

To live and die in love.
To have a song in your heart
but your voice is heartlessly out of tune.
To swim while drowning
in an unrequited monsoon.
To lie and repent
with each breath you consume.
To journey to hell
but be heaven sent too soon.
To gouge your eyes out
but ask to see.
To listen to the waves
but cry out that each wave ends your
misery.

Black girls are life.
Yet, Black girls think about death
as if life is hardly a choice.

REB

She wept in the most beautiful of ways.
Tears created pools in the single dimple of her cheek.
Her eyes widened larger than any moon I'd ever seen
and her lips…
Her lips were but silken gates,
enclosing sincerity from jaw and speak.
When she convoked the courage to concede,
I'd hear the melody of her whispers
saying:

please pardon me.
I lost discernment but now I see
that I am worth more than the prison
you created for me.
Captive to your insecurities
what a fool to believe
I was worth anything less than

free.

IRTH

Convincing myself that I am not lost,
suppressed my essence in the name of love-
Never to return.
Lost in a new world of repentance and pain.
Looking for evidential hope
for remnants of myself
to lead me back to myself.
Quenching his needs
I nearly washed away my light.
I became anchored and chained.
Holding my head above the waves,
I wondered
if love is like water,
why am I drowning in shame?
If love is like water,
why do I not enjoy the rain?
Drinking from his reserve
yet drinking in vain.

I want to pray for everyone who finds love in the form of lust. For women who gift their hearts and bodies to men who will never love them. For men who give parts of themselves to women who will never see them whole. For women who prey on fortunate men. For men who indulge on fruitful women. For men who find love in convenience. For women who disassemble women to build up men. For men who break down women with dishonesty. For those who foolishly think this is love.

Memo to self

Secrets don't make it easy to write.
Lies don't make it easy to love.
Fear don't make it easy to fly.
Baby, you are a writer that loves to fly.
Put your feet on the ground,
pencil in hand,
write words that'll take you far.
Farther than distant lands
in your dreams.
In your reality,
be fearless,
be brave.
Be all that you desire to be.
Love hard.
Love righteous.
In your darkest of days,
Promise me one thing:
Continue to write.
Be fearless
and fly
And, always
love honestly.

Parcel denied

You are love letters never opened.
Beautiful emotions penned to paper,
preserved by the seal of an envelope.

It's the quiet dreams you keep to yourself. The fortune in your pocket. The delicate whispers under your breath. Returned moments almost forgotten. It's the smile from across the room. These are all the ways in which you are reminding yourself to stay aligned with your purpose. Listen to yourself. Pause in those moments. Live in them just enough to excite yourself to continue creating, loving, and growing into the best version of you.

Never will I regret the changes
I have gone through
to grow into the butterfly I am
becoming.

LEARNING TO BE STILL WHILE LEARNING TO LOVE THE IN BETWEEN

Every day I pray. Every day I cry. I am vulnerable, yet my strength is the prelude to invaluable smiles and passionate embraces. I endured depression and won. At night, I still dance with tears in my eyes. The last of years were the hardest and the happiest. I lost love. I found freedom. I realized that love after love exists and even in that understanding, I know my love may not be perfect, but my heart is all in. I fell in love with an alchemist. We create. We love, but I love with urgency as if eternal isn't tangible and tomorrow isn't guaranteed. I glory in our eternal moments because love is patient. And, I am ok with this because love is not self-seeking. Love always hopes, always perseveres. My heart is heavy. My smiles are heavier. I live my purpose. My purpose is bigger than any selfish desire. I will change my community. I will change the world, starting with changing me. I stand by that. I stand by my faith. I cry out in praise. I cry out in fear, yet I am a fighter. I declare, I am not perfect.

I wondered why I am always sleepy.
I get a full night I sincerely confess.
I lay my head on my pillow
and caress my hands against my chest.
It's not my body that needs comforting,
it's my heart that needs rest.

I pray I understand this.

I am love. I am worthy to be loved. I am the poetry I write. I am each word on its best day and each word on its worst. I failed. I tried again. I've fallen and enjoyed the fall for longer than I hoped. Enjoyed sorrow and silence being voiceless and compliant. I have risen. That is me no more, crying I am here. Listen to my cries.

Understanding 2
Love After Love
After Love

Memo to self

There is power in loving after love.
An immeasurable amount of strength
grows from the choice to get back up again.
To decide to plant your own flowers,
to decide to bloom
and glory in the garden you created.

The fire in her angelic eyes-
Mesmerizing.
Yet, alluding to a power she never knew,
never could command,
never knowing her worth.
The very same cloud covering her confidence
created false confidence.
She'd hide behind it,
cry in silence,
creating an unnatural defiance.
Her mere presence was created to create
yet she simply existed
melancholic,
falling from the heavens like melodies,
sobbing rain down on me.
Yet, ironically her pen was all dried up.

Memo to self

I read your words.
Your blades.
Your honesty.
I wasn't prepared for your shoddy cursive.

Flowing strokes of funk and blues
with history at my back.
 Penning pages to undo
 a life I once regret.
 Foreordination must explain
 a life of loss and pain
to grow and know
 a seed craves the soil and the rain
but when the waters over pour
we lose sight of its course
and drown in thought of returning to
a life we once remorse.

From time to time,
I write these words
with a pen that has no ink.

It was sometime in July, before I traveled to Los Angeles, that I felt a tingling inside of my chest. I wasn't sure what it was, but I knew it was worth looking into. I made a doctor's appointment to further review. I thought it was butterflies fluttering or nerves that I allowed to get the best of me, but I had to know for sure. The doctor asked me to touch my toes, nose, and further supposed that maybe quite possibly, I swallowed a seed. I walked away from that appointment so confused. I eat healthy. I'm sure I swallow seeds all the time and not one made me feel this way. Later that night I prayed about the seed I swallowed hoping the feeling soon passed. God told me, "My dear, you swallowed a seed, a seed that was a dream. A dream that you are now blooming inside of you. You feel uncomfortable because growth is uncomfortable, but the bloom my child is beautiful."

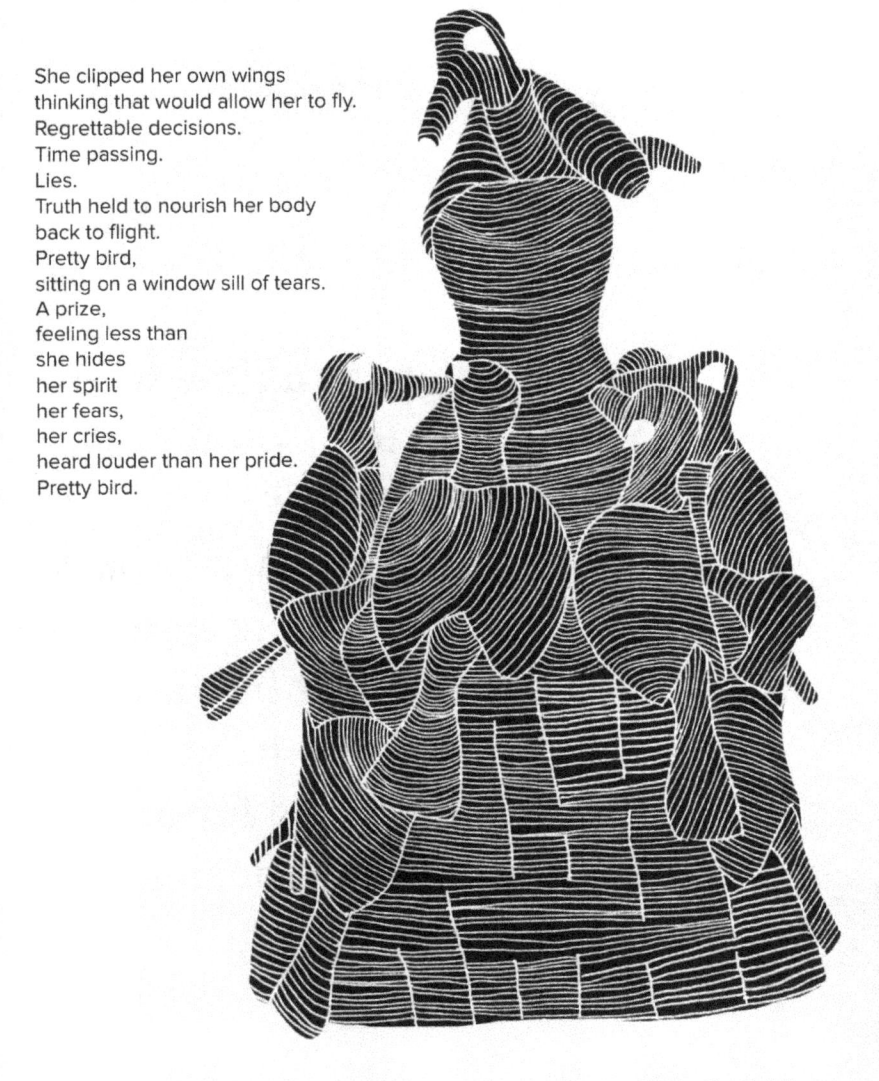

She clipped her own wings
thinking that would allow her to fly.
Regrettable decisions.
Time passing.
Lies.
Truth held to nourish her body
back to flight.
Pretty bird,
sitting on a window sill of tears.
A prize,
feeling less than
she hides
her spirit
her fears,
her cries,
heard louder than her pride.
Pretty bird.

Losing love ain't easy.
Losing self is worse.
Finding love is worth it.
Realizing it was you all along,
is the answer.
This pretty bird now flies.

It is important in a time where we are fighting to be on the right side of history, that we also fight for ourselves. We take a step back. We remove ourselves from the calamity and chaos of the times, to hear our own need for healing and acknowledge that need for others. In order to be strong in the fight, we must be healed. We must whole.

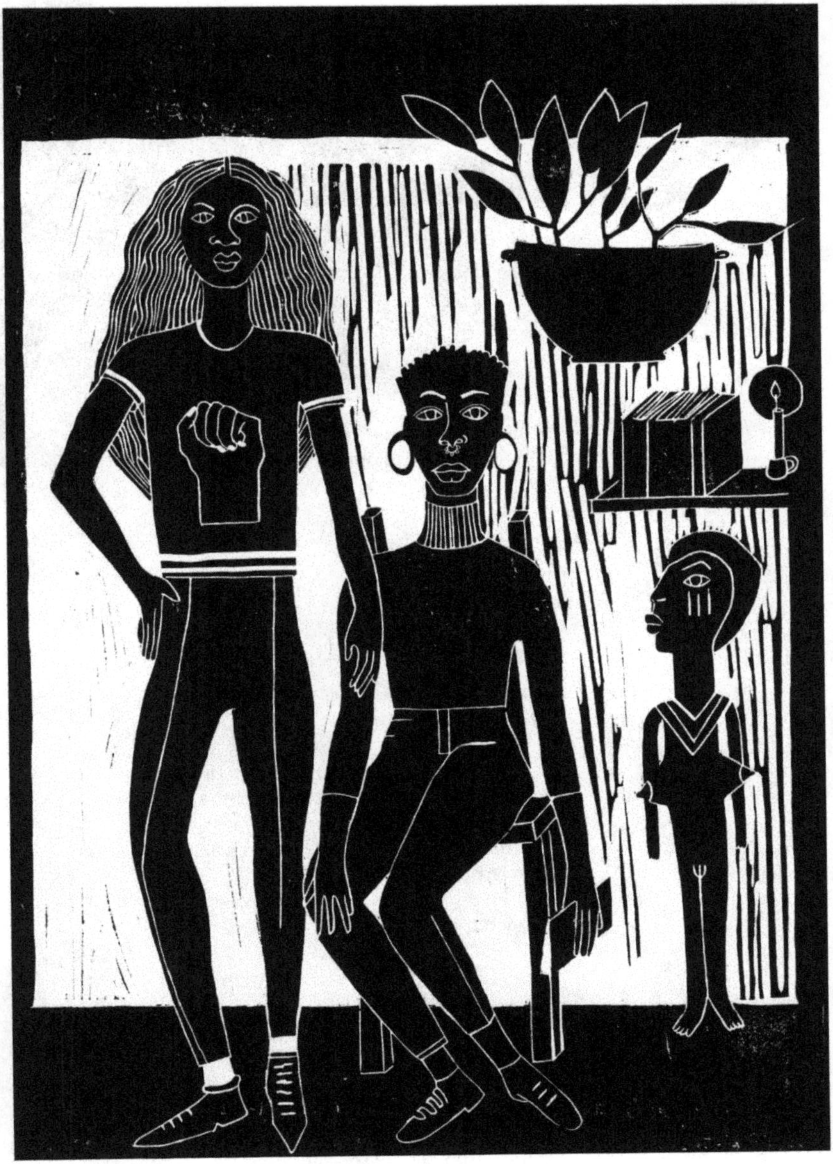

When they say blue on Black bodies
I imagined the midnight's moon
finding comfort on our layers of legacy.

Not this.

Creating shades most can only dream of.

Not this.

When did hate become a color?
Has it always been?

'Cause it seems like injustice and disdain
was birthed by men who don't shine
under the moonlight.
By men who choose not to comprehend
or maybe they do.

They do.

They know we grow from the richness of
God under the sun
and we dream of triumph under the
moon.

We gon' glow regardless.
They try to take our light
but we gon' glow regardless.

Let Our People Grow

GROW
GROW

Griot

I am healed.
I am healing.
I promise to always to always be.
I am love.
I am loving.
I promise to always dream.
I am hope.
And always hoping
to live life
as a love revolutionary.
I am the lesson
and I am learning
to always honor my calling.

I HAVE BOOKS INSIDE OF ME THAT WILL BIRTH NATIONS

I HAVE A

> I no longer quantify dreams as big or small. I just dream.

DREAM

Phonetic stories of freedom

I am the result of a dream.
Not just dreams conceived by me
or countless scenes crossing memories
of that only a parent can foresee.
It was many dreams from my ancestors
who often had nothing else but.
I am because they did.
I bloom but not all on my own.
I was but a seed.
A collection of tears
fell into fields of dreams
and watered me.
I grew into a mighty oak,
with roots that run deep
to reunite me with where it all began.
My roots still speak to me.
So, if you see me in the trees
native to resilience and majesty,
know that I'm listening
for the whispers of ethereal beings
who sacrificed their lives for me.

She was most beautiful
when she let go of inhibitions,
self-doubt,
and worry.
She made room for magic.
She made room for discovery.
She made room for long reads,
writing from her soul,
and painting from her heart.
She made room for faith.
She was most beautiful when she
made room for
her.

A dreamer once dreamt of being as
good as him, her and they.
I still dream that dream
however, for now
I am happy just being good at being me.
So, I'll dream that dream
as I lay my head to sleep,
until the stars unite the night
and the sun awakens me
'til I am one with the moons
and two souls united as one.
I'll dream that dream
'til the world rests easy
and that dream is done.

DEAR RADICAL WOMAN,

Keep walking.
    Throw your worries to the wind.
Closed eyes open third views to within.
    See what's there
What's always been.
    A love inside you that ain't easily won.
They will try but won't win.
 A heart that frees prisoned boys to become men.
    A love that don't compare to the revolving doors they used to.
    You not them.
 Exhausting yourself to prove that you not them.
    Be patient with love.
    Be patient with you.
    Being alone ain't a loan of your body
    to every man that's withdrawn
from honoring women like the mothers before him.
You don't owe them.

MY UMI SAID

Black women write poetry.
We feel.
We cry.
We smile when no one is watching.
We are both the dreamers and the dream.
We sit under the sun,
charging our melanin
from the richness of God.

The earth is heavier than the sea

I am the strength in my poetry.
I am the light in my smile.
I am the hope in my eyes.
I am the bend in my back.
I am the fruit of the earth.
I am the strawberry against your lips.
I am the sun.
I am each ray against your skin.
I am the moon.
Call me Luna.
I am its glow.
I am each star you wish upon.
I am the very essence of your favorite Black movie.
I am the lyrics to the song that won't escape you.
I am your favorite childhood memory.
I am the universe.
Beautifully called:
Black woman.

Not every angel
wears a halo
above their crown.
Some wear it in
the beauty of their
melanin.
Heaven rests easy
on em'
like chiffon,
pastels and soft
tones.
Neon blues and
jazz moans.
Rouge smeared lips
and Sunday's best.
Buck jumping and
undulating hips.
2 jobs and eviction
notices, hustle and
flow
ain't got nothin' on
em'.
Marching bands
live in their bones.
They've got
dissonance in their
roar
with majestic
undertones.
Echo their names
across your lips.
Caress their wombs
with resonance.
They birth nations
with backbones.

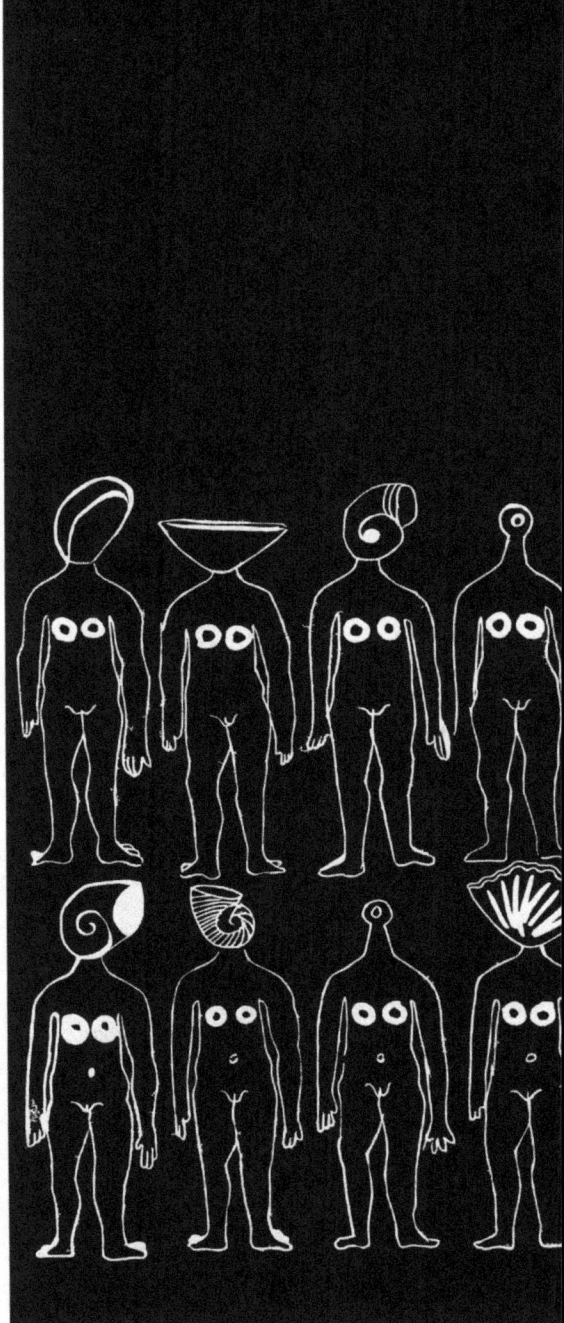

How to Make Black More Palatable:
A Beginner's Guide to Loving Black Coffee
and Black Tea-
Please stop trying to sweeten me

---

1 cup of innocence
2 tablespoons of melanin raw
1 teaspoon of dried jasmine
3/4 cup of brown skin under the moonlight
7 kisses from lips like melons
a dash of sage
4 talks of revolution
2 teaspoons of cocoa butter
1 Black on Both Sides album
1 book marked to the chapter of Angela Davis

You Are The Recipe

You grow from what you feed yourself. Feed yourself love. Feed yourself confidence, honesty, and the parts of heaven you can reach. Feed yourself a good book, the arts, wonder, and all that you consider challenging. And, when you've consumed enough and can't possibly consume anymore, glory in the fullness of those moments; because hunger will come in the morning.

EXIST OUTSIDE THE LINES.

Find courage on the edge
where inspiration meets freedom,
where love meets you,
where your past becomes a roadmap
unfolding ambition overdue.
Dividing like tightly folded origami.
Revealing art out of the things you lose,
the lesson is in the loss.
Know the artistry is still there.
It's in the cross you carry
and the smile you choose to wear.
It's in the tears that fall,
watering your evolution and bloom.
The ambition is always there
because your ambition, my dear, is you.

We make sand castles out of desire, building dreams that were never meant to last. Desire without purpose and prayer blow away like sand in the wind. Castles crumble and we wonder how we got there. Be purposeful and prayerful in your build. Take your time. Plan well. Inspiration lies across the reach of your hand. Feel the love where you stand. Mantras in the sand.

The sun poetically dances on my skin,
fostering an aureate light of love.
Reminding me that last night,
you gave me a smile
that will forever remain.
A smile I pray will always stay
like 25 hours in a day,
summer rain against my window pane,
pecans from my grandfather's yard,
catching Wild Tchoupitoulas Indians in the Tremé.
Corner stores,
big shots,
and beignets.
Eating red beans after Mondays.
Playing dominoes on Tuesdays.
And, cornrows in my hair for picture day.
Please stay.
I wouldn't have it any other way,
but for your smile
to live in my sweetest
memories.

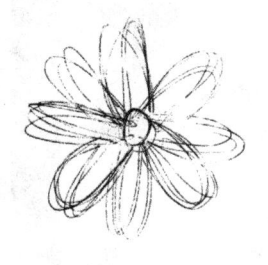

Summer's end

Choosing tapes to play in my father's music box.
Sitting on the block with the sun against my back.
Detangling telephone cords.
Racing to the corner where we double dutch in the wind,
'til the beads on the ends of our braids spin
and the beads on my neck tell stories of how my summer was
without groom.
Making gumbo out of pinecones and mud from my
grandmother's recipe.
She cooked up imagination.
From golden to brown,
the school kids who lacked my glorious melanin
would always wonder where I've been and who I am.
And, without question
I would tell em'
I am the sun
moon
and the stars in between.
I exist outside of expectations
in a summertime breeze.
Where words lie in the trees
creating the most rhythmic poetry
and the streets tell stories of my freedom
'til the lights come on.

RAMBLE YOUNG GIRL RAMBLE

A man once called me a "whole woman". I was smitten by my understanding of those words together. I've been a good woman, an interesting woman, a beautiful woman, and many words in-between, but to be seen as a woman whole means everything to a woman who was once broken.

Treat my heart as such

I was created by the Most High. The same Creator who made mountains out of ideas and filled land with water calling them oceans and shores. I was created by the same Creator that shaped clouds to comfort the skies and stars to brightly shine through the night. I was created by the same Creator that handcrafted the heart and placed it between both lungs, knowing life is defined by many things, but in the melody of each beat it's the freedom in each breath, and the love that pumps from the crowns of our heads to the tip toes of our feet. I was created by the same Creator that handcrafted the endearing warmth of a touch. That created the human body not to be confused with the soul that makes us who we are. He created that too. I was created by the same Creator that gave His life for the lives of humans who would not be so humane. He died for me. So, when you look at me and wonder why I value myself the way that I do, remember I was created by the same Creator that created you.

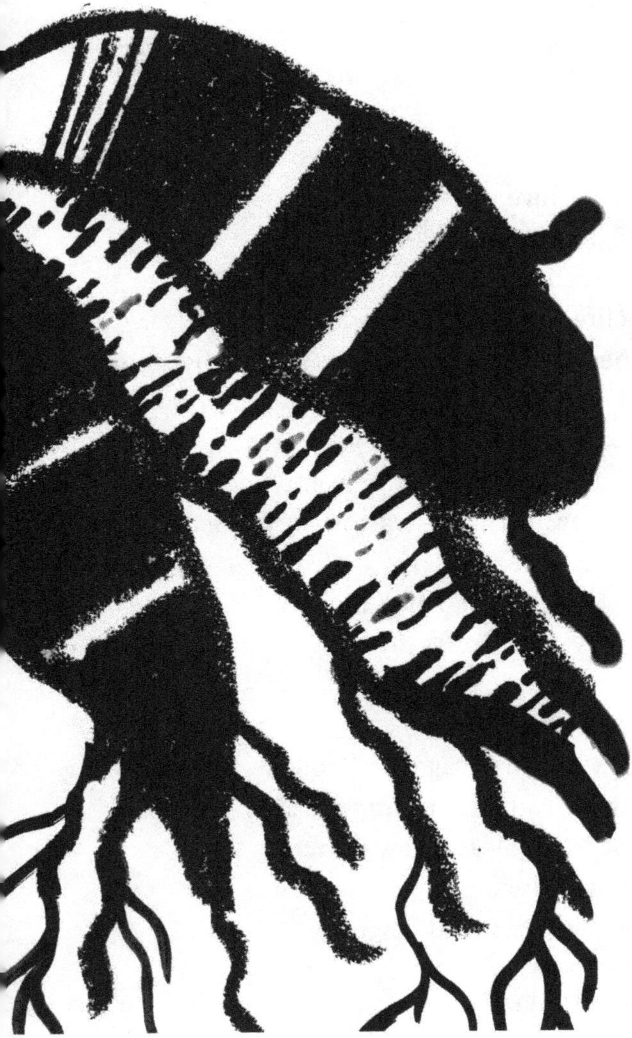

ODE TO GWENDOLYN BROOKS

To be in love,
is to put flame to hand.
To be reborn through the delayering
of a life of love never lived
or never lived up to the love you are living.
To be in love,
is to feel a feeling not of your own.
To know his heart is warm and body is cold.
To cover him in the warmth of your soul.
To be in love,
is to taste the charm of his lips
yet leave sweetness to savor.
To be in love,
is to know pain.
To set sail on voyages unknown.
To find beauty in sinking warships.
To be in love is to know God.
To know glory.
To know fate in a stranger.
To be in love
is to know you.

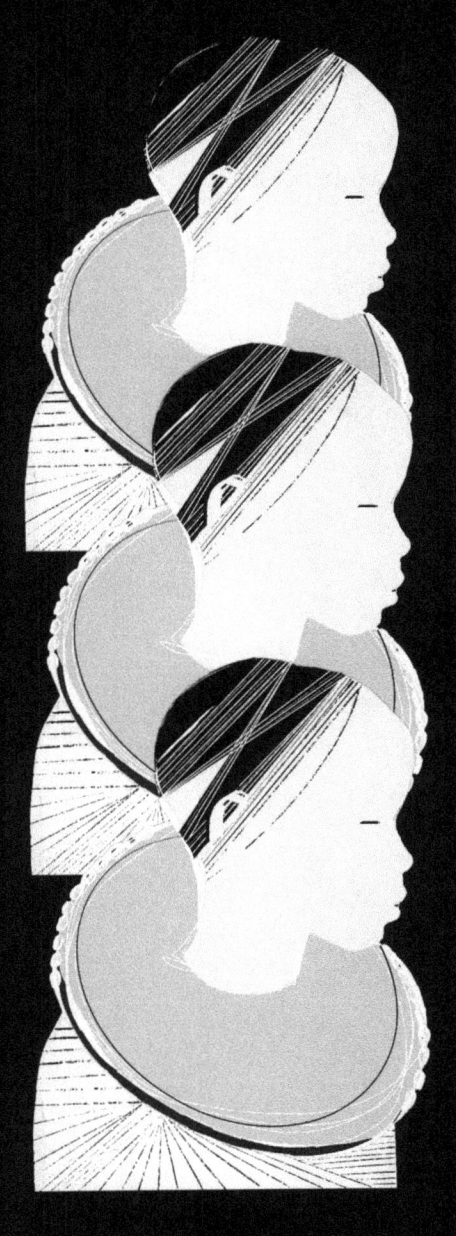

Intentional lover.
Intentional love.
I choose you.
I choose you, every day.
I choose to pray for you, when I wake, to my God for the heaven's sake,
for the lost boys who look to you for escape.
I pray for you for the heaven's sake
for your time and travels, that they be safe,
for the energy you welcome and the hands you shake,
for the life you create and the change you paint,
for the hate you heal and the love you make.
I pray to my God for you for the heaven's sake.

I crave you in the most innocent of ways.
I crave to say good night
after your longest of days.
I crave to lay my head on your chest
and hold hands as we sleep
our nights away.
I crave to listen to your worries
and pray they never stay.
I crave to tell you how I will always adore you
for forever.
Forever

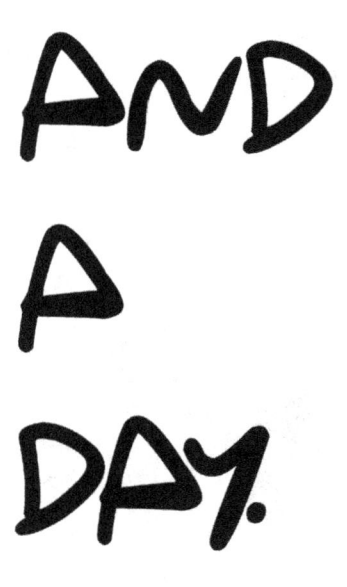

AND

A

DAY.

As of late I challenged my beliefs on love. I truly desired a deeper understanding of it all. Truth is, I believe in love. I believe in a God-ordained kind of love. The kind of love that makes you say *I do* when God says *it's already been done*. I believe in a love that is patient. A love that will wait for you. I believe in a love that is understanding. The kind of love that listens. I believe in a cosmic kind of love. The kind of love that shifts time and space to make time in space for you. I believe in a love that revolutionizes the idea of what we once thought love was. I believe in a love that inspires. A love that creates hours that feel like seconds, and seconds that feel like days. And, without a doubt I believe in partnerships and friendships filled with that kind of love.

My thoughts are
often prayers.
So, know that if I'm
thinking of you,
I am more than
likely praying for
you.

He whispered, be patient with me.
I may not be ready but I want to be

Meanwhile

I'm ready for a love that shouts for me.
But I love the way it whispers
when I'm with you.

RAMBLE YOUNG GIRL RAMBLE

MUSE

She stared intensely at my art
and I couldn't help but think that she was mine.

I passionately whispered,
make love to me.
Embarrassed by the request that parted my hips,
the foolish words that escaped my lips
and each tear wiped by your fingertips.
You grabbed my face and whispered,
we are already making love.

She lifted her nose from deep inside of her book to glance towards him. From that moment on, he knew the most beautiful women are those that write poetry.

Words his heart whispered that his lips could never speak

Infatuated by the whim of a chance,
the unforeseen occurrence of a brief meeting,
I captured her beautiful face in a photo.
Manifesting the recurrence of her gaze, .
I stared until I saw her face no more.
I now see her soul.

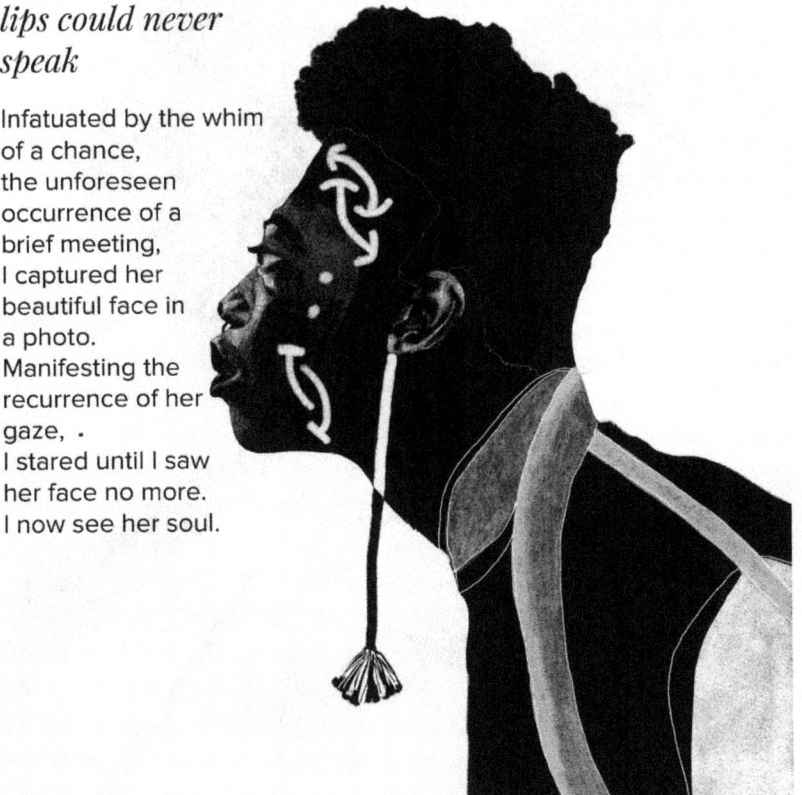

And though I see her face every day,
I still find beauty in her asymmetrical lines.

When I see you,
I see sunshine.
I see rays.
I see a future beyond the sunny
days.
I see rain.
I see clouds.
I see frightening lightning
displays
and even in those darker days,
I wouldn't have it any other way.

Sometimes I feel like my soul met its mate,
like happily comes after
and love is my fate.

Your smile is what caught my eye. Inviting me in. Comforting me. Convincing me that a kiss was necessary. The rest is history, or maybe the present, and quite possibly the future. No telling though. So, we take each moment as a reminder that love isn't textbook. The events that brought us together aren't any less special than the story we write moving forward. I see the way you look at me. I know you love me. I also know you are cautious. Because what could be any less predictive than a love that isn't textbook?

> Today I found tomorrow in your smile.
> Meanwhile, you found a smile I thought I lost forever.

ME? FEEL YOU

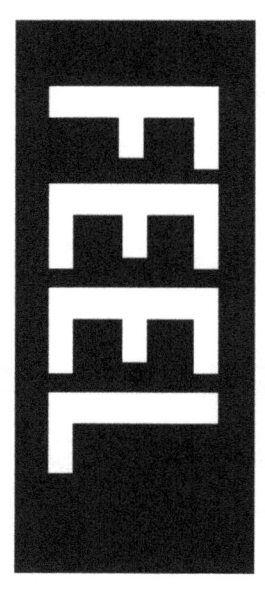

Bold words from shy lips.
I was made for you.
Like clay from you
I was made from you.
I prayed for you
and pray for you.
Wrote scriptures of love like psalms
only we could sing
sweet melodies from heaven
only God can bring.
I was made for you.
I'm sure of it.
I lay my lips between your conscious
and unconsciously kiss your ego.
Closing our eyes,
drifting to a serenity only we can go,
assuring you that it's perfectly ok to love me.
It's ok to love me
and hold me.
And, hold me.
Make love to me.
Console me.
It's ok.
Because I was made for you.
It's ok to want you,
to want you as much as I do,
to want to learn from us,
teaching me all the ways we can be.
It's ok to want to be your poetry,
To write your wrongs,
recite your dreams
paint your hopes,
to be the eternal to your ephemeral.
It's ok to want forever
even if it doesn't exist.
Bold words from shy lips.

Last night you asked me what are stars

It's 2am. I don't sleep much. Life has changed. To the point where 2am's feel like 1pm's and the stars just don't compliment the
night. They've become my entertainment of sorts. It's 2am. I lay
counting each one. Wondering what life would be like if I said no more often. If I said yes to loving me. The window doesn't seem large enough to see all the stars so I press my face against it as if that would make a difference. Rubbing my eyes, I wish upon each
wonder and what if. I wish that I never wonder and what if again. Each road taken has made me into who I am. Each failure a lesson.
Each failure learned from. And so, each star isn't just a star, but a reminder that God gives second chances, lessons are learned, and life goes on.

He asked me if I ever think of him.
I responded,

"YOU ARE MY 2PM PRAYERS AND, MY 2AM THOUGHTS."

*Who would've ever predicted
that our bodies would align in a way
that would make the stars jealous.*

TO THE MAN I LOVE

The man plus his art created the artist.
Without the man, the artist does not exist.
The art will always exist without the man,
as an untouched idea
or moments found in the stars, on earth, and
emotions that run through our bodies,
like blood through the inferior and superior vena cava.
The art will always exist.
The art is necessary.
The man.
The man is the creator.
The man exhausts himself to create the art,
reliving eras the world chooses to ignore,
coercing him to call on his ancestors for advice,
for history books never revealed.
The man understands that his art is bigger than him.
That it slightly shifts the earth with each stroke,
moving mountains,
shaping ideas.
Its beauty alone forces those who gaze into its existence
to fall deeply in love.
But where does that leave the man
lost in his creation?
Depleted.
Lost in the necessity to create
because the art is necessary.
Who is the man without his art?
That man is you.
You are supernatural.
Extraordinarily great.
Wise.
Resilient.
Educated.
Your smile was divinely created.
You revolutionize the world with love,
manifesting an unassailable desire for the closest thing we
humanly know as a love so supreme.
You are Black.
You are our history.
You are our present.
You take for granted nothing
because you are excellence.

>You powerfully exist with or without your art.
>You are the creator.
>An alchemist.
>A manifestation of your own destiny.
>You are love.
>And, you are loved.

I AM WOMAN

Watch the beauty that occurs
when you begin to love with your eyes closed,
allowing love to just be.
No expectations.
No judgements.
No titles.
Just two souls
wandering in the direction of forever.

I fell in love with *a man*
who painted me.
He painted *colors of hope*
onto a canvas of possibility.
He saw the sunset in my *eyes*
and the sunrise in my heart.
He's *forever mine* as I know it
and I, forever his in his *art.*

Walking the streets counting heartbeats.
Children jumping hopscotch bare feet.
Wishes blown from my lips like dandelions in the wind.
Dreaming of cold cups and days when I was them.
Not a care in the world.
Hard to care for this world.
Prayers for this world.
Graffiti on the walls.
Looking over my shoulder.
I found you.

You painted wings-
>   Now I fly.
Painted me religiously-
>   Baring your soul,
you gave it your heart.
Now, my love runs endlessly.

When the person you are with inspires you to smile more,
recognize that feeling as love. In the last of years, I opened my
heart to a man who expanded my understanding of want and need.
His friendship challenged my stagnant pace. Over time, I fell in
love with him. Within his embrace, I knew creativity was no longer
a muted want, but a roaring need. My faith strengthened and my
purpose became clear. I saw God in him because God lives in him.
And though I am all these things in his absence, I smile because he
smiles. I love because he is love.

TWIN FLAME

Burn baby burn

Love will not only set your soul on fire,
it will ignite a passion inside you
that cannot be put out.

SOUL MATE

Your soul startled me.
Moved me in a way
that excited me.
Breathing new breath into a lifeless
vessel,
you ignited me,
setting wildfires to old dreams
that were once put out by
regret.

Hold me

You hold me in arms that remind me of my father.

Though you taste different each time that I kiss you,
like honey, your lips are the sweetest reprise.

Your kisses linger days over,
keeping my heart full
and my body satisfied.

I wrote these words in your arms

We wake:

I lay beside you listening.
Head on your chest,
hoping to sync each breath with mine
I stop breathing to catch your rhythm
but never can.
Well, I can and I do, but uncomfortably so
maybe I was not made to be your whole.
As if breathing in sync meant just that,
your exhale in my ear is as soothing as waves crashing onto shore.
In your arms I feel the peace most dream of.
So, I lay in your arms and just be,
realizing that each breath I take fall between yours.
I smile because as I exhale, I make us whole.

We rest:

I run my fingers along your face as you sleep.
Feeling the very strength I see when I look at you,
hoping to remember each groove and dimple.
Hoping to remember it well enough
that I never doubt it with my eyes closed.

Love is where the art is

I read somewhere that art and love are the same thing. I further interpreted that to mean that it is the process of seeing yourself, or the ability to see beyond yourself in things that are not you, and that is powerful indeed.

We oughta be praying for more days like this.
You know, I'm convinced earthquakes are made of our laughter.
The kind of laughter that shakes the earth
and the way we part our lips to smile and grin.
Well that may be how land parts from land.
Making the kind of islands people dream of vacationing,
they'll relax on our smiles.
Imagine that.
We oughta be praying for more days like this.
The kind of days that turn into nights,
revealing hope in our eyes.
The kind of hope that'll light up a city night sky,
like a fleeting star
they'll make wishes on our love.
Imagine that.
You know I'm certain
the way we hold hands
bring people together.
Tangling nations,
they'll call it unity.
Imagine that.

If I love you,
I've asked you to pray for me
and pray with me.
I've boldly made the first move on embrace.
I've held your hand.
Hoping each line sings our story
of how palms created psalms and sweet symphonies.
I've listened to you
and tasted the sweetness of each word.
Creating confection out of the sincerity of your soul.
I've been vulnerable with you.
I've cried with you.
I've laughed with you.
I've created memories that I will always hold onto.

I should've kissed you longer
because the weekend seems too long
and your embrace feels too far.
Your smile seems to fade.
I hear your voice in imaginary tones.
You breathe fiction.
I read between the lines.
Hoping each breath proves fact
to your bones in my closet.
Hoping each release
proves that you were once here.

We stand on borrowed time.
Falling in love with hope.
Creating forevers out of ideas
that we could actually be together.
That every second is hours
and ours is perfectly ok to say
and feel
and feel
and feel.
Our minds forming forevers
beyond the silhouette of our bodies,
pressed against the window pane
that temporary is as permanent as we want it to be.

Mic check 1, 2

You're stuck in my head like a melody
unchained.
Making rhythms out of seeing your smile.
Holding your hand.
Lying beside you.
Kissing your neck,
only to see you again today.
I can make a habit out of you
like a memorable tune
flowing from my lips,
I can sing about our love all day.

Ode to Nina Simone

Oh Nina,
Mamma said they'll be days like this.
Oh why are there days like this?
Prayers don't help days like this.
Praying woman I art.
Selfishly relying on my Black magic to conjure you back into my life.
Oh Nina,
your upright proud Black man spine
sending chills down my poet's pen.
Causing me to write about this unrequited love
backslider I art.
Sinnerman once again.
Oh Nina,
just love me or leave me.
Never standing in your shadow.
Keep me
forever by your side.
Lips ajar on your forbidden fruit,
tasting your soul
feeling oh so good.
How can I exist without you?
Oh Nina,
when I love to love you,
caressing you is like Memphis in June.
You got my soul at peace,
yet my body out of tune.
Putting a spell on me
you got me screaming,
Mississippi goddam.
Somebody say a prayer.
Praying woman I art.
Lost in your world
and only you can save me.
Restore me.
Behave me.
I warn you.
Oh Nina,
everything must change.
You lay my hopes down
but tell me don't smoke in bed.
You caress my fears

and forget about the sweet nothings you ever said.
Oh Nina,
I need you to be more than an instability,
an unrequited passionate possibility.
Don't play me like your ivory.
I am more than just your keys.
I wish I knew how it feels to be freely in your arms.
Until then…
I'll indulge on this lilac wine
as these tears roll down my cheek,
staining music sheets
creating loveless soliloquies.

NINA SIMO

Will you hold my hand and pray with me?
Pull me close and stay with me?
Rest your soul and lay with me?
Take a chance and parlay with me.
Love like jazz Coltrane with me.
In the streets, we dance and sing.
Songs of love and hope we bring
a future brighter than anything.

I want to be jazz with you.
Playing it by ear
as our bodies make beautiful music together.

Brotha knew I had a way with words,
a poet of thoughts.
Rhymes vibrating from my lips
like the sweet sound of Black people's laughter.
We exchanged words before exchanging words.
He, an artist too.
Showing him the surface of me
he asked me to go deep
when all I could think of was him going deeper.
Soul deep.
So deep.
Getting lost in his thoughts deep.
Soul deep.
So deep.
Getting lost in my arms deep,
yet finding himself in my rhymes.
Allowing me to undress his mind deep.
Brotha knew I had a way with words
and he an artist too.
Appreciating his art is like seeing his soul.
The very essence of him is love.

After much anticipation,
I disrobed for him,
removing expectations,
revealing silhouettes and smiles.
I told him stories of
what will be
and to his surprise,
I didn't remove the obvious.
I showed him my purpose
and revealed my calling.

I want my name to live on your lips,
in ways that cause you to say it when you think of love.
In ways that weigh on your every thought,
making you wonder what love was before me.
I want to love you long enough to see your grandfather in you,
in ways that turn boys into men,
in ways that carry your smile into the wind.
Making the world around you curve its lips
into the purest kind of grin.
The kind that forgives the most indecent of sins.
The kind of smile that says endings are beginnings and I see you.
I want to create realities out of your dreams.
So even after your longest of days when you cannot sleep,
you'll think of me and rest easy knowing my love is comforting.
I want to lay my head on your shoulder while you sing sweet symphonies
of how we created a love so beautifully
out of kinship and honesty.
Oh, the resonance of our harmony.

Eat me in,
eat me out
leaving soul residue on your lips.

From the nape of my neck, down the arch of my spine, your lips grace my warm brown skin, manifesting an unassailable desire for the closest thing we humanly know as a love so supreme.

He found the
universe in her
hair,
when all she
wanted him to
find was her heart.
To be openly
loved
without
conditions.

Ancestral rhetoric

Baby girl, you can make a Black man blush.
Stripping hard exteriors and street conditionin'
callus hands and thickened skin.
Shells of what we call preservation.
Layers of history layered in love.
Hardened coverings melt away at the smile of you.
Feet that marched the streets of Michigan in 1963 and '62
and he ain't never been out of the south.

My mama would call him a man of men.
Ancestral excellence of the men before him live on his tongue,
shouting, we have overcame and we shall overcome.

And, you…

Your story lives on gilded edges,
reading chapters of change,
familiar as psalms sung on a Sunday.
Bellowed in negro spirituals ushered in the wind.
Swing low and promised lands,
he prayed for you.

Manifesting the women before him.
Before him,
you exist
lifted on high,
you exist.
Birthing nations,
you exist.
You are our strength.

Our revolution will not be televised

Your heart speaks revolution.
My love speaks evolution.
In that combination,
there's no substitution.
We have a revolutionary type of love.

Communities carry us in healing.
Purveyors of truth audacious and bold.
Our love spoken with oral pen,
predicted and foretold.

Jumping brooms
as culture serves reminders of our past.
Blessing us with strength of nations
and unions that outlast.

The world will ask about our bond.
Streaming love poems far and wide.
We'll shy away from thoughts of fame.
There ain't no hesitation in our reprise.

There will be no re-run sisters and brothers
'cause love is the revolution.
Our revolution will not be televised.

Goodnight moon

Read my worries a lullaby
and I'll write your body a love scene.

>   I've been told I'm hard to read
>   and I remind em'
>   a good book will always make you question.

Like the past was a dream
and the future a distant memory.
The future me will either be with you
or over you.
Either way,
I will be amazed at how the current me
is caught up in your smile.

Class in session

The idea that loving you may be a lesson, is
disheartening.
Imagine every time I say, I love You,
you think of teaching me otherwise.

Pride is her name

I came to you with words of truth,
hoping to protect your name.
You dismissed my proof
and chose to make me the one to blame.
I never deceived and won't start now.
Her lies you found comfort in.
The truth is hard.
She'll never admit
the deception she placed you in.
Perhaps, it's deceit that entices you
and honesty reminds you of love.
Proud Mary

As a child, I found transcendent joy in bedtime stories and prayer before saying goodnight. Around 8 o'clock, we'd gather around the bed to give thanks and serenade farewell requests in the most innocent tones. Our prayers were composed, but imaginative almost as if they were stories, we told God. We prayed for peace. We asked for guidance and adventure. We prayed for purpose. Our prayers remind me of the sweetness of home.

Years later, I still appeal for those things, but I now pray for discernment above all else. I live unfettered by law. I live to love freely and honestly, but none of those work tooth for tooth if a smile don't have teeth and if eyes don't have the wisdom to see that everyone ain't free and most don't live honestly. In a world where truth is freedom, dishonesty is as comforting as the forgiveness that follows. It's 11 o'clock and I need discernment more than ever.

My heart was disappointed by a man who chose not to believe the free and honest love I forced upon him. Maybe that's it. Maybe forcing love and honesty on him was like forcing a child to pray at night with no imagination and he wasn't a child. He was a man of men. A man of the future who lives beyond words of truth because he too lives truth. Maybe I should've allowed him to discern for himself like I did for me. Perhaps I took away his freedom.

For the first time, I think living freely and loving honesty, may have cost me a love that felt like 8 o'clock prayers filled with imagination. A love that felt like telling stories to God. A love that felt like home.

What is a greater tragedy
than a love that never lasts.
Perhaps it wasn't God that day.
I wish I would've asked
if it was the truth He told
or whispers from my past
that presaged stories of love
or a pain that would outlast.
So, now when I pray,
I question my faith
and beg emotions never start.
It's better to protect a love never lived
than mend pieces of a broken heart.

Kiss M
Baby
One

I want to grow old with someone who once knew me young. Someone who saw my inner journey begin and end with lines that tell stories of we have overcame and we shall overcome. I will see them as literature. The world will call them wrinkles. And in time, we will see their beauty. I want to grow old with someone who once saw my coils drape the sides of my cheek. From silk wrapped around my locs and the way I change my mind in between. To wired hair that sits full of life and gray. Someone who still appreciates my curls as they lay. I want someone who loves the way my body has changed. Who reads between the lines on my thighs. Who knows beauty is deeper than skin and lovely bones. Music sheets and tethered strings to hearts that beat in synchronicity with melodies written before them. I want to grow old with someone who has survived many lives with me. Who lives to be reborn. Who sees the rising of the sun as renewing. And, the departure of each moon as God's sweet amnesty.

To Be Continued ...

Me More Time

Sometimes, I feel like I am only practice for you.
You ask me to come over and we put in more practice.
They say practice makes perfect
and all I ever wanted was a love to call perfect.
Yet, the time in between kisses I feel deserted.
The time in-between talks I feel burned
by your flame.
By our flame that once was
we were lit.
We are lit.
You leave me in the shadows of the unknown.
You leave me in the unknown alone
because you know
you're not ready.
But you are ready for me to come over.
We both run into each other's arms,
making this love feel more like practice.
Practice makes perfect.
All I ever wanted was a love to call perfect.
Maybe what we have is worth it.
Baby, don't desert it.

To the lover I gained along the way

You got a mother's love out of me.
The kind that cares eternally.
The kind of love that nourishes your very being.
That knows
you are worth more than your worst moments
and your greatest memories.
The kind that protects,
feeds the soul
and the body.

Dear lover:
You got a lover's love out of me.
The kind that mends a broken heart,
sewn delicately into the pages of her poetry.
The kind that knows
the curve of your lips
ain't always a smile
and your embrace translates to
love, hope, and uncertainty.
The kind that finds your humor unforeseeable
and 5 seconds from funny.
Your alchemy intriguing
and your love overdue.
The kind that makes groceries at 1am
and scrambles eggs on French bread,
the way your grandmother taught you.
The kind that traces the lines against your face
when you sleep
and you read between her lines,
finding shelter in unhoused emotions
when she speaks.
The kind that is willing to work on love.
Heal scars.
Heal nations.
Stop wars.

Dear lover:
I will forever love you.
Even if I truly don't know how.

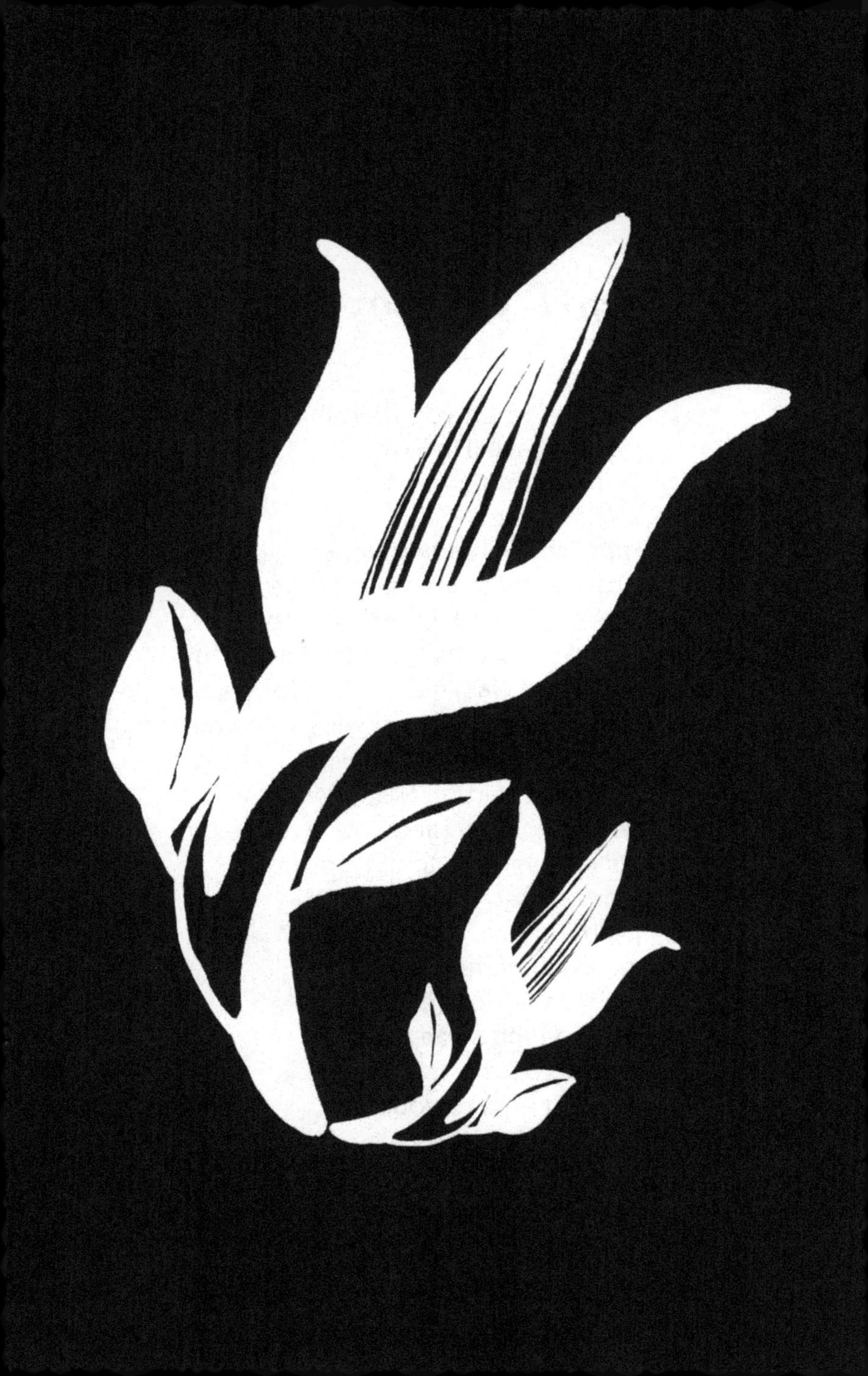

1-504-355-1095 - sing song

Call me when you read this poem.
I think I'm still in love with you.
I wrote some words
It feels unreal
that I'm not holding hands with you.
The last thing said before we broke
was that you'd let me read to you
poetry of proofs that need no proof.
That love was in the plans for you.
Now I'm not making plans with you.
Distant tongues from all that's true.
I left my heart on 92,
where you decided you love me too.
It's always hard to say goodbye.
Maybe,
perhaps
we don't have to.
So, turn the page
and see me soon,
by your side
reading next to you.

As the Most High is my witness, one of the best feelings is love.

AUT

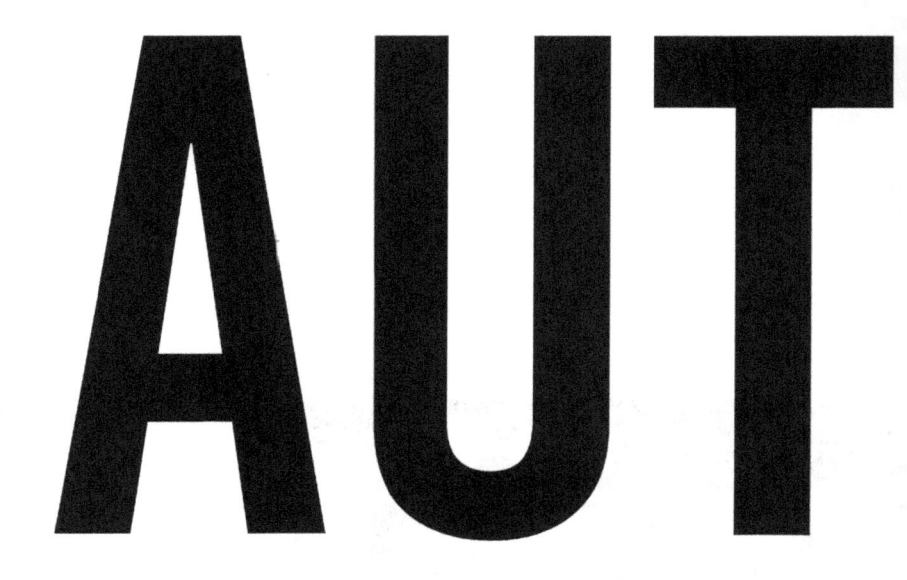

HOR

New Orleans born and raised, Monique Lorden understands the power of poetry and storytelling. She weaves ancestral rhetoric and proclamations of freedom and revolution into rhyme, verse, and runs. Mother of two and stranger to none, Monique's poetry feels like kinship. It is a gentle reminder from a family friend that we have overcame and we shall overcome.

CPSIA information can be obtained
at www.ICGtesting.com
Printed in the USA
LVHW021423141021
700428LV00002B/238